Raghav Trivedi is a barrister at St Philips Chambers in Birmingham, specialising in commercial and chancery law. He holds a particular specialism in property law, insolvency law and wills, trusts and probate matters and cross-border issues in these areas.

A Practical Guide to Conflict of Laws Issues in Property Disputes

Jurisdiction and Applicable Law

A Practical Guide to Conflict of Laws Issues in Property Disputes

Jurisdiction and Applicable Law

Raghav Trivedi LLB (Hons), LLM
Barrister and Mediator, Inner Temple,

Law Brief Publishing

Published 2026 by Law Brief Publishing, an imprint of Law Brief Publishing Ltd
30 The Parks
Minehead
Somerset
TA24 8BT

www.lawbriefpublishing.com

Paperback: 978-1-918241-37-2

To my family, for their endless support, encouragement and belief in me – standing by me through every challenge and obstacle life has thrown in the way.

PREFACE

As a junior practising barrister specialising in commercial and chancery law, I have been lucky and privileged enough, in my six years of practice to date, to have been trusted by my Instructing Solicitors to deal with a number of cases which has involved a complex foreign element. Naturally this has, time and again, required me to thoroughly research into the world of private international law commonly referred to as the conflict of laws in order to deal, and engage, with the issues of my clients.

It is through this process of research and a dedication to grasping and understanding the complexities associated with conflict of laws principles where I found my love for the conflict of laws subject and its intricacies, technicalities and underlying policies and principles. It is on that basis that I completed, with Distinction, my Masters in International Commercial Law to broaden my knowledge and develop my skills in this area of practice. It is also on that basis that I have found the courage and the stamina to write this book.

As I have traversed the vast legal commentary in this area of law over a number of years, I have come to learn that the principles of conflict of laws are not necessarily easy for a fast-paced legal practitioner to read and digest. Given that the area of conflict of laws deals with the interrelation of legal systems between different sovereign states, the principles which govern this interrelation can be convoluted with numerous rules and principles and exceptions to rules and principles.

This book therefore serves a particular need and function. It is a non-exhaustive practical guide, with key practical tips and takeaways, for the fast-paced legal practitioner who requires a reference point in their research for their cases to deal with the issues of their clients dealing with foreign immovable property. This practical guide does not deal with *all* of the points and principles but only some of the main ones. The reader is directed to specialist practitioner texts in this area of law for further details when preparing their cases.

Further, the principles of conflict of laws do not operate in a vacuum. There are conflict of laws principles applicable to many areas of law such as, *inter alia*, tort, contract, property and insolvency. I have particularly encountered conflict of laws issues arising in the context of contractual disputes in relation to immovable property (i.e. real estate and land) located abroad. Therefore, in order to avoid superficiality and promote specificity, this practical guide deals with conflict of laws issues in the context of property disputes where the immovable property is located abroad (outside England and Wales, Scotland and Northern Ireland). It is also dealing with only two particular branches, namely jurisdiction and the applicable law (and within the branch of applicable law, this book specifically deals with contracts relating to rights in rem in foreign immovable property and transfers of foreign immovable property). The practical guide is therefore aimed primarily for a practitioner that deals with property disputes albeit there is a particular significant overlap with contract law as the reader will see.

I would like to first and foremost thank my parents for their unwavering and unconditional support in all of my endeavours throughout my life, including in the creation of this book. Without them I would not be in the privileged position that I am in. I would also like to thank St Philips Chambers for graciously opening the door and giving me the opportunity to showcase my talents as a barrister without which I would not have been given the opportunity to write this book. I also thank each and every former supervisor and mentor of mine from St Philips Chambers, each one leaving an indelible mark and influence on me professionally and from whom I continue to learn and grow in my practice.

The law set out in this book is correct and up to date as of 14 April 2026. This book sets out the legal position as it relates to proceedings begun, and any contracts entered into, following Brexit after the end of the transition period for the UK leaving the EU on or after 1 January 2021.

Raghav Travedi
April 2026

CONTENTS

CHAPTER ONE

INTRODUCTION

The Concern of Conflict of Laws or Private International Law Principles

The natural question to ask before considering the detail of this book is: what is private international law and the conflict of laws. Firstly, the terms private international law and conflict of laws can be used interchangeably and refers to the same thing, namely a set of rules and principles in private, often commercial, cases that come into play when the case contains a foreign element. The reference to conflict of laws is therefore a reference to a situation where, due to the existing foreign element, the laws of one country come into direct conflict with the laws of another country. The aim of the conflict of laws principles is therefore to help decipher the nature of the conflict and resolve the same.

The Nature and Content of this Book

This book is a non-exhaustive practical guide for legal practitioners dealing with a property dispute where the foreign element is the land or real estate (i.e. the immovable property) located abroad. This book deals only with the position relating to foreign immovable property outside England and Wales, Scotland and Northern Ireland. Ultimately, if the legal practitioner is presented with this type of legal problem it is important to take a step back and break down the order of analysis of the conflict of laws principles to ascertain appropriate next steps, strategy and prospects of success.

Firstly, the legal practitioner must consider the issue of jurisdiction. This is the fundamental issue which must be considered to determine if the claim *can and should* be issued in, and heard by, the Courts of England and Wales. Chapters Two through to Five look at the issue of jurisdiction in the context of a property dispute where the property is located abroad (i.e. outside of England and Wales, Scotland and Northern Ireland). In particular these Chapters will delve into the meaning of jurisdiction, the general rule of jurisdiction when the dispute involves property located abroad, the exceptions to the general rule and what other jurisdictional requirements must be satisfied to establish the Court's jurisdiction in these matters.

Secondly, the legal practitioner must consider the issue of applicable law. Once a case is in the hands of the Courts of England and Wales, the Court will be required to apply the appropriate law to the facts of the case. In a case involving foreign immovable property, the question is what law is to apply to the dispute in hand. Chapters Six through to Eight looks at the issue of applicable law in the context of a property dispute where the property is located abroad (i.e. outside of England and Wales, Scotland and Northern Ireland). In particular these Chapters will consider the conflict of laws principles at play to determine the applicable law where the dispute involves a contract relating to property located abroad (i.e. outside of England and Wales, Scotland and Northern Ireland) and the applicable law relating to transfers of foreign property interests plus the principles and rules behind pleading and proving foreign law.

Thirdly, the legal practitioner must consider the issue of recognition and enforcement of judgments. Once the Courts of England and Wales have decided the case, the question then becomes how that judgment is to be recognised and enforced abroad in another country. This third issue is outside the scope of this book given its depth and complexity and which may require its own practical guide in due course. However, legal practitioners should always be aware that by obtaining a judgment in England and Wales, this does not guarantee that it will be recognised and effectively enforced abroad or alternatively it may prove to be time consuming and a costly exercise. This issue must therefore be carefully considered at the outset of any analysis. Nonetheless, the reader will see that the issue of enforcement does crop up, now and then, when considering the issue of jurisdiction and applicable law.

The Three Branches of a Conflict of Laws Analysis

The reader will note that there are essentially three branches when dealing with a conflict of laws analysis, namely jurisdiction, applicable law and the recognition and enforcement of judgments. Whilst the branches do overlap and it is easy to get confused or conflate these three separate branches, each branch must be treated separately in any analysis of any case with a foreign element. Jurisdiction is the key that unlocks the door to the Court, the applicable law is the substance that the Court applies and the recognition and enforcement of judgments is the means by which the Court's decision is given real-world effect and value. Each branch symbolises an important aspect of any conflict of laws analysis that will allow the legal practitioner to determine if the case is one worth pursuing or not.

This book deals with the first two branches in the specific context of a dispute involving foreign immovable property located outside of England and Wales, Scotland and Northern Ireland. Any reference to *foreign immovable property* or *immovable property located abroad* is to foreign land and real estate and any reference to immovable property *located abroad* is a reference to a location outside of England and Wales, Scotland and Northern Ireland.

This book sets out the legal position as it relates to proceedings begun, and any contracts entered into, following Brexit after the end of the transition period for the UK leaving the EU on or after 1 January 2021.

CHAPTER TWO:

THE INTRODUCTION TO AND THE GENERAL MEANING OF JURISDICTION

The term jurisdiction is a term which is often used by lawyers and appears a deceptively simple term. Whilst overlapping, a particular clear distinction must be drawn between two uses of the term as set out below.

The first use of the term jurisdiction is in a physical sense referable to a particular territory where a Court has the power to compel parties to be brought before it. For example, it might be said that an individual within England and Wales is within the jurisdiction of England and Wales. Indeed CPR r 2.3 confirms that jurisdiction means, unless the context requires otherwise, England and Wales and any part of the territorial waters of the United Kingdom adjoining England and Wales. Further, CPR Part 6 Section Two refers to the service of the claim form in the jurisdiction and Section Four refers to the service of the claim form and other documents outside of the jurisdiction of England and Wales. One can see the use of the term jurisdiction as referable to physical location in a particular territory where the Court's power to compel parties to be brought before it operates.

However, whilst the aforementioned use of the term is important to place parties within the boundaries of a particular legal territory and understand whether proceedings ought to be served within or outside the particular legal territory, for the purposes of the principles of conflict of laws there is a more prominent use of the term jurisdiction, namely referring to the Court's power to entertain proceedings in England and Wales by compelling parties to be brought before it. The question here is whether the Court has the power to deal with a particular case at all (i.e. whether the Court has jurisdiction over a particular party and case). In other words, jurisdiction here is the key that unlocks the door to the Courtroom and, where a foreign element is involved, this is the first thing that the Court needs to establish in order to hear the matter at all.

Looking at the meaning of jurisdiction in this latter and more prominent sense, there are two important sub-questions. The first is whether the Court has the power to compel the party to be brought before it to deal with the matter in question at all. This is the question of the existence of jurisdiction. The second is whether or not the Court ought to exercise the power. This is the question of exercise of jurisdiction. This was neatly summarised by the High Court in ***IMS S.A. and Others v Capital Oil and Gas Industries Limited*** [2016] EWHC 1956 (Comm) ("**IMS**") at [27]-[28] as follows:-

> "*It is well known that in the context of challenges to jurisdiction, reference to the Court's jurisdiction can be a shorthand for two different concepts: one is the Court's jurisdiction to try the claim on its merits; the other is the Court's exercise of its jurisdiction to try the claim (see, for example Hoddinott v Persimmon Homes (Wessex) Ltd [2007] EWCA Civ 1203, [2008] 1 WLR 806 at [28]). Leaving aside cases covered by the Lugano Convention and recast Brussels 1 Regulation, service of process is the foundation of the Court's jurisdiction to entertain a claim in personam, and accordingly the Court has such jurisdiction only where the defendant is served, in England or abroad, in the circumstances authorised by, and in the manner prescribed by, statute or statutory order (typically the Civil Procedure Rules): see Dicey Morris and Collins The Conflict of Law 15th ed. Rule 29. Where there has been no such service, the Court does not have jurisdiction. Where such jurisdiction has been established by service of process, the Court may*

nevertheless decline to exercise its jurisdiction, for example on grounds of forum non conveniens or lis alibi pendens" ([27]).

"The two types of challenge are logically and juridically separate and distinct. Moreover they typically involve different forms of relief. Where there has been no valid service necessary to found in personam jurisdiction, the Court will set aside service and set aside the claim form. On the other hand where the challenge is to the exercise of jurisdiction on grounds of forum non conveniens, the appropriate relief is usually a stay of proceedings, which is capable of being lifted, if appropriate in the light of subsequent events" ([28]).

The above demonstrates that the issue of the existence of jurisdiction is largely governed and determined by the application of the service rules contained in CPR Part 6 and the principles that have stemmed from the same. The Court's power to entertain proceedings in England and Wales is determined on the basis of service of proceedings bringing a party within the jurisdiction of the Courts of England and Wales. This is usually not controversial where a party is located in England and Wales and is able to be served inside the jurisdiction in accordance with CPR Part 6 Section Two and Practice Direction 6A. However, where a foreign element is involved, it is likely that a party will be required to be served with proceedings outside the jurisdiction given the nature of the dispute and the likely location of the defendant outside England and Wales. CPR Part 6 Section Four and Practice Direction 6B governs the rules applicable to service of proceedings outside the jurisdiction. In other words, the Court only has power to compel a party to be brought before it to try the case if, *inter alia*, that party has been validly and effectively served. The rules and principles of jurisdiction are examined in full in Chapters Three to Five.

However, as set out above in IMS, even if the defendant has been validly and effectively served and the existence of the Court's jurisdiction is satisfied, this may not be the end of the matter. There may arise the second sub-question, namely whether or not the Court's jurisdiction ought to be exercised (i.e. whether the Court should compel a party to be brought before it to try the case). This sub-question is likely to come into play in one of two circumstances – the first is where a defendant is validly and effectively served in the jurisdiction of England and Wales but challenges the Court's jurisdiction by arguing that the Courts of England and Wales is not clearly the appropriate forum to bring the claim (known as *forum non conveniens*) and the second is where the claimant seeks permission to serve proceedings outside the jurisdiction of England and Wales which requires the claimant to also satisfy the Court that England and Wales is the proper place in which to bring the claim (see CPR r 6.37 (3), known as *forum conveniens*).

These requirements of jurisdiction (specifically in the context of property related disputes where foreign immovable property is located abroad) will be examined in further detail in Chapters Three to Five. This will examine the key rules, principles and law applicable to the aforementioned service requirements under CPR Part 6 and challenges to the existence and exercise of jurisdiction under CPR Part 11.

It is always important to bear in mind that the principles relating to jurisdiction differ to the principles governing the law that applies to a dispute where a foreign element is involved. Just because an English Court has jurisdiction does not necessarily mean that English Law will be applied to the dispute at hand where a foreign element is involved. The principles relating to applicable law is dealt with in Chapters Six to Eight.

Summary of Key Practical and Tactical Tips

- It is important to understand the meaning of jurisdiction, not just as the location or territory of the Court, but as the power of the Court to compel a party to be brought before it to try a case.

- It is important to maintain a separation between the existence of jurisdiction and the exercise of jurisdiction. The existence of jurisdiction is the existence of the Court's power to compel a party to be brought before it to try a case whereas the exercise of jurisdiction is the Court's use of the said power.

- Equally, it is important to maintain a separation between two sub-questions that arise from the meaning of jurisdiction as the power of the Court to compel a party to be brought before it to try a case. The first sub-question is whether the Court can compel a party and try a case and the second sub-question is whether the Court should compel a party and try a case. These are distinct questions with different tests and remedies to be applied. This will be considered further in Chapter Five.

- However, service of proceedings is the basis upon which the Court's jurisdiction is partly founded. If service is not validly effected, the Court's jurisdiction falls away. It is important to ask whether the defendant has been properly and effectively served under CPR Part 6. One must carefully identify at the outset whether the case is a 'service in' or 'service out' case. Equally CPR Part 11 governs the procedural rules for challenges to jurisdiction and works in tandem with CPR Part 6 (and can be analysed in a single framework). This is considered further in Chapter Five.

- If confronted with the question of whether the Court should compel a party and try a case, it is vital to understand whether you need to mount the argument that England and Wales is the proper forum (*forum conveniens*) or whether you are faced with the argument that England and Wales is not the proper forum (*forum non conveniens*). The detail of this is considered further in Chapter Five.

- It is important to understand the implications of different challenges to the outcome. If a defendant successfully challenges jurisdiction on the grounds of *forum non conveniens*, the Court is likely to stay proceedings. If a defendant successfully challenges jurisdiction on the grounds that no jurisdiction exists because there has been no validly effected service, the Court is likely to set aside any order granting permission for service and/or set aside the claim form. The detail of this is considered further in Chapter Five.

- Do not confuse jurisdiction with applicable law. A Court may have jurisdiction but apply foreign law to the case at hand. It is important to keep this distinction clear in any analysis of a case with a foreign element.

- It is also important to anticipate a jurisdictional challenge in any case with a foreign element. For example, in the context of this book, property that is located abroad.

- Jurisdiction is the first port of call in any analysis of a case with a foreign element. One must remember that if jurisdiction is not established or there is a successful challenge, the claim fails at the outset with potential heavy costs and time wasting consequences. Understanding and anticipating jurisdictional issues from the outset will prevent these consequences coming into fruition.

CHAPTER THREE

THE GENERAL RULE OF JURISDICTION IN RELATION TO FOREIGN IMMOVABLE PROPERTY DISPUTES

The Foreign Property Context

Now that the reader has an understanding of the general meaning of jurisdiction, that meaning must now be given the context of a dispute between parties related to foreign immovable property. The first question, in these circumstances, is whether the Courts of England and Wales has jurisdiction (i.e. the power) to compel the parties to be brought before it to try this type of case. This is the existence of jurisdiction question in this context.

The General Rule from Moçambique

Chapter Two examined the general meaning of the concept of jurisdiction and some of the key principles and rules to be applied in determining the question of jurisdiction (to be further expanded in Chapter Five). However in the foreign property context identified above there is a particular qualification when it comes to the existence of jurisdiction question. That qualification is derived from the age-old but leading authority of ***British South Africa Co v Companhia de Moçambique*** [1893] A.C. 602 ("**Moçambique**") which sets down a very specific exclusionary rule at common law that the Courts of England and Wales do not have jurisdiction to determine the title to, or the right to possession of, foreign immovable property ("**the Moçambique Rule**").

The Moçambique Rule typifies and gives effect to a general conflict of laws principle that can be found across the world, namely that where the case involves immovable property, the Courts of the country where the property sits has exclusive jurisdiction over it. As the reader will see when examining the principles of applicable law, this general principle ties in neatly with the general principle of *lex situs* (namely that the applicable law to a dispute involving foreign immovable property is the law of the country where the foreign immovable property is physically located).

As can be seen from the above, the Moçambique Rule places a special qualification on the jurisdictional principles applicable to cases involving foreign immovable property. If the cause of action concerns the title to, or the right to possession of, foreign immovable property then the Courts of England and Wales holds no jurisdiction and cannot entertain the proceedings. The reference to title to, or the right to possession of, foreign immovable property is essentially a reference to rights held by a party in the foreign property *in rem* (i.e. against the whole world). These are a reference to proprietary rights. This is significant, for the reasons to follow in the next Chapter, because the Moçambique Rule is only a very specific exclusionary rule and is subject to a few exceptions.

The Rationale for the Moçambique Rule

The reader will have noticed that the Moçambique Rule dates back to the late nineteenth century and this common law principle has continued to remain in place. However, what is the rationale behind the rule? The rationale was examined and explained in ***R Griggs Group***

Limited and Others v Evans and Others [2004] EWHC 1088 (Ch) ("**Griggs**") as follows:-

> *"Suppose the dispute concerned land outside England, instead of copyright. Except where they felt able to exercise their equitable in personam jurisdiction (see below) the English Courts refused to decide questions of title to foreign land. This was so even if the defendant was otherwise properly before the English Court. In the first instance, it would have been pointless to assert such a jurisdiction: how could our Courts order foreign peace officers to put the successful claimant in possession of the land? In the second place, they considered that to try title to foreign land would have been disrespectful to their foreign judicial colleagues, as by seeming to undermine their jurisdiction and authority "* ([**62**]).

> *"At various times several reasons have been advanced in justification of the Moçambique rule. In my judgment the only rationale which survives today (apart from the Court's possible incapacity to execute its order abroad, which is not applicable in our case) is that it would be a breach of international comity to try questions of title to foreign land in rem, save incidentally: see, for example, the judgment of the Court of Appeal in Pearce v Ove Arup Partnership Ltd [2000] Ch 403, 430d. But we still have to discover precisely why it would be considered a breach of comity"* ([**72**]).

As can be seen from the above passages, the Judge in Griggs starts with the conclusion that the rationale behind the Moçambique Rule is that, even if a defendant is brought properly before the Court (i.e. the general rules of jurisdiction have been satisfied including the valid and effective service of proceedings – see Chapter Five), when it comes to rights in rem in relation to foreign immovable property, from a practical perspective the Courts of England and Wales are not in a position to enforce and execute its judgment in respect of the same directly. However, from a policy perspective, the Moçambique Rule is justified on the basis that to try questions of title to, and right to possession of, foreign immovable property, this would be disrespectful to the authority of the foreign Courts and in breach of, what is called, international comity (i.e. a principle of respect and deference to the laws, rules and procedures of a foreign state). Indeed, because the foreign immovable property is seated physically in the territory of a foreign state, one can see why a foreign state may be offended if *rights in rem* were tried and tested by the Courts of another foreign state. This ties in neatly with the principle of *lex situs* discussed earlier (i.e. the general principle that the applicable law in relation to a dispute involving foreign immovable property is the law of the country where the property is seated). However, the Judge in Griggs went further:-

> "*It cannot be merely because, in trying title to foreign land, we would be delving into a right of property which is granted by and exists under the laws of a foreign sovereign. For instance, it is clear that no equivalent to the Moçambique rule has ever applied to chattels. They might be ships, or jumbo jets... Yet nobody objects that the bringing of the action is forbidden because it may call into question the existence or scope of laws created by a foreign sovereign. The foreign law is treated as a question of fact. The foreign law is created at the will of the sovereign, and, when we find the fact, we are trying to respect his will, not defy it*" ([73]).

> "*Hence it must be clear that the proper justification for the Moçambique rule cannot rest on a general proposition that our Courts do not entertain disputes concerning the existence or scope of laws made by a foreign sovereign. They do it all the time*" ([74]).

> "*So the reason it is perfectly in order for our Courts to decide that the defendant has misappropriated or dispossessed chattels situate in a foreign state, contrary to the laws of that state; to decide that the defendant is liable for personal injuries or damage to property inflicted by his breach of the local road traffic or ship navigation*

> *laws; to decide that A but not B shall succeed under an English will made by the owner of foreign land; to order that X must convey to Y land situate in a foreign state in accordance with his obligation, must be because, according to the usages of nations, it is not considered to be a breach of comity to do these things"* ([77]).

The Judge here is questioning why the case of trying the title to, or rights to possession of, foreign immovable property is met by the exclusionary Moçambique Rule whereas this same exclusionary rule does not exist when it comes to, for example, other forms of property rights relating to chattels and other causes of action. The Judge notices that the Courts frequently do delve into foreign property rights in this respect and entertain disputes concerning the existence and scope of foreign laws all the time. Yet there is not considered to be a breach of comity in this respect. However, by way of this process of reasoning and questioning, the Judge reaches the following conclusion:-

> *"Even so, it is apparent that to litigate a title in rem to land situate abroad is regarded as a special case. Why is it a special case? It is partly because the Court cannot enforce its judgment and partly because it is felt the local sovereign might object. But why might he object? Why can one bring a claim that says "According to the laws of the sovereign the chattel is mine", but not "According to the laws of the sovereign the land is mine"? The answer must be that it is understood that in the case of land the sovereign is or may be asserting a double prerogative. It is not only a prerogative to make laws for his own country, but a prerogative to have those laws adjudicated in his own Courts exclusively. That was the traditional understanding when it came to land"* ([78]).

From the above, it is clear that the Judge was not convinced as to why the Moçambique Rule has held a special place in the common law distinct from the approach taken when it comes to other areas of law (such as chattels and conversion). However, the Judge appears to settle on the position that, in relation to foreign land, the nation state is asserting a double prerogative that it makes its own land law and, when it comes to proprietary rights in rem, the Courts of its own country holds exclusive jurisdiction in relation to the same.

Summary of Key Practical and Tactical Tips

- It is important for the legal practitioner to identify from the outset whether the claim is going to engage the Moçambique Rule. If the matter concerns title to, or rights to possession of foreign immovable property, the Courts of England and Wales will decline jurisdiction (however this is subject to the statutory modification applicable to causes of action involving tort, explored in the next Chapter).

- Whilst the detail of exceptions to the Moçambique Rule will be considered in the next Chapter, the legal practitioner may want to consider how to frame the cause of action so as to avoid engaging the Moçambique Rule. The Moçambique Rule is triggered squarely when the case deals with proprietary rights in rem in relation to foreign immovable property. However if the claim being asserted relates to rights in personam this may be permissible (as explained in the next Chapter). It is the effective and proper characterisation of the claim which will likely prove decisive in at least moving pass the jurisdictional hurdle of the Moçambique Rule. It is therefore important to focus on the nature of the right that is being asserted.

- It is therefore also important to undertake an analysis of the case to see how it can be framed, anticipating the need to rely on the exceptions to the Mozambique Rule (as explored in the next Chapter) as early as possible. Where the Moçambique

Rule is engaged the focus ought to shift to see whether any of the recognised exceptions explored in the next Chapter apply.

- When dealing with foreign immovable property, the Moçambique Rule provides for a special jurisdictional rule that can easily be missed. It is important for the legal practitioner not to assume jurisdiction simply because the general rules of jurisdiction are otherwise met and the defendant is before the Court. Even where service of proceedings has been validly effected, the Court may still lack jurisdiction if the claim engages the Moçambique Rule. It is equally important to not assume that, just because Courts routinely adjudicate disputes involving foreign law (including in relation to personal property) that this is the same when it comes to foreign land. Foreign land is a special category of case as set out in this Chapter.

- It is vital to understand that the Moçambique Rule deals with the existence of jurisdiction and is an absolute exclusionary rule. Once engaged the Courts of England and Wales lack jurisdiction altogether and it holds no discretion to assume jurisdiction otherwise.

- By engaging with the Moçambique Rule, as set out above, as early as possible the legal practitioner can avoid adverse consequences for their client such as the strike out or stay of the claim, adverse wasted costs orders and the duplication of proceedings abroad on the same subject matter (i.e. the proprietary rights in rem).

- The analysis and application of the Moçambique Rule to the case at hand ought to sharpen the picture of the horizon ahead for the client. For defendants the Moçambique Rule can be used as a powerful jurisdictional objection and for claimants it can be used as a factor in shaping or framing the claim. Unless an exception to the Moçambique Rule (explored in the next Chapter) is engaged it may be that proceedings abroad are inevitable. Even if an exception is engaged, other considerations may be brought to the forefront, namely the recognition and enforcement of judgments and the costs of enforcement and execution depending on the location of the property. Enforcement against foreign land may be ineffective or commercially not viable.

- The crux of the above is that the Moçambique Rule is not just a mere technical limitation but a strict limitation which is a fundamental expression of territorial sovereignty and international comity when it comes to immovable property located abroad. The expression is rooted in the ability of foreign states to make land law and for their Courts to exclusively adjudicate in relation to proprietary rights in land. The limitation ties in with the *lex situs* principle which points to the primacy of the law where the property is physically situated. It is a limitation that must be confronted at the very outset of any cross-border property dispute.

- Examples of the types of cases that might fall into the Moçambique Rule include possession proceedings in relation to foreign land and disputes over title and ownership of property (and any relief in support such as injunctive or declaratory relief).

CHAPTER FOUR

THE EXCEPTIONS TO THE GENERAL RULE OF JURISDICTION IN RELATION TO FOREIGN IMMOVABLE PROPERTY DISPUTES

The Exceptions in Outline

As set out in the previous Chapter, whilst the Moçambique Rule is an absolute exclusionary jurisdictional rule where a case deals with the title to, or rights to possession of, immovable property located abroad, there are certain exceptions. This Chapter examines those exceptions.

The first exception is where the case is really dealing with the contractual relationship or equitable rights between the parties, ("**the In Personam Exception**") and the second is where the Court needs to determine title to, or the right to possession of, foreign immovable property for the purpose of administering an estate or trust that deals with a mix of foreign and domestic property ("**the Trusts and Estates Exception**").

Thirdly, pursuant to Section 30 (1) of the Civil Jurisdiction and Judgments Act 1982, the jurisdiction of any Court in England and Wales or Northern Ireland to entertain proceedings for trespass to, or any other tort affecting, immovable property shall extend to cases in which the property in question is situated outside that part of the United Kingdom unless the proceedings are principally concerned with a question of the title to, or the right to possession of, that property ("**the Torts Exception**"). However, whilst outside the scope of this book, the reader should be aware that the Torts Exception is subject to the provisions of Schedule 4 of the Civil Jurisdiction and Judgments Act 1982 (see Section 30 (2)). It is the above exception which has led the Supreme Court in ***Lucasfilm Limited and Others v Ainsworth and Another*** [2012] 1 A.C. 208 to state the following:-

> *"It is clear that much of the underpinning of the Moçambique rule...has been eroded. All that is left of the Moçambique rule...is that there is no jurisdiction in proceedings for infringement of rights in foreign land where the proceedings are "principally concerned with a question of the title, or the right to possession, of that property""* ([**105**]).

Whilst the aforementioned quote appears to target the Moçambique Rule generally as opposed to the Torts Exception specifically, as the reader will see below, a claim under the In Personam or Trusts and Estates Exception will not, by its very nature, be principally concerned with a question of the title, or the right to possession, of foreign immovable property.

The In Personam Exception

In the Privy Council case of ***Pattni v Ali*** [2006] UKPC 51, Lord Mance stated at [**26**] that:

> "*it has long been accepted in England that an English Court may, as between parties before it, give an in personam judgment to enforce contractual or equitable rights in respect of immovable property situate in a foreign country.*"

Further in the Court of Appeal decision in Moçambique ([1892] 2 Q.B. 358, **364**) this exception was explained in the following manner:

> *"Courts of Equity have, from the time of Lord Hardwicke's decision in Penn v Lord Baltimore... exercised jurisdiction in personam in relation to foreign land against persons locally within the jurisdiction of the English Court in cases of contract, fraud, and trust..."*

In other words, so long as the general rules of jurisdiction have been satisfied (see Chapter Five), the Court has jurisdiction to preside over a case dealing with the enforcement of contractual or equitable rights in respect of foreign immovable property (e.g. a case involving breach of contract, allegations of fraud and breaches of trust to name a few). The Court can give an in personam judgment in relation to the same. Whereas a judgment dealing with proprietary rights in rem deals with the rights over immovable property against the world, a judgment dealing with personal rights in personam is a judgment dealing with the rights and interests personally existing between the parties alone (e.g. contractual or equitable rights and interests).

However, it would appear that this exception is not a narrowly contained exception and could apply to a wide variety of cases involving personal obligations which could be enforced. The Judge stated the following in ***Deschamps v Miller*** [1908] 1 Ch. 856, **863-864**:-

> *"The question is whether under these circumstances the Court ought to entertain jurisdiction. In my opinion the general rule is that the Court will not adjudicate on questions relating to the title to or the right to the possession of immovable property out of the jurisdiction. There are, no doubt, exceptions to the rule, but, without attempting to give an exhaustive statement of those exceptions, I think it will be found that they all depend on the existence between the parties to the suit of some personal obligation arising out of contract or implied contract, fiduciary relationship or fraud, or other conduct which, in the view of a Court of Equity in this country, would be*

> *unconscionable, and do not depend for the existence on the law of the locus of the immovable property. Thus, in cases of trusts, specific performance of contracts, foreclosure, or redemption of mortgages, or in the case of land obtained by the defendant by fraud, or other such unconscionable conduct as I have referred to, the Court may very well assume jurisdiction. But where there is no contract, no fiduciary relationships, and no fraud or other unconscionable conduct giving rise to a personal obligation between the parties, and the whole question is whether or not according to the law of the locus the claim of title set up by one party, whether a legal or equitable claim in the sense of those words as used in English law, would be preferred to the claim of another party, I do not think the Court ought to entertain jurisdiction to decide the matter."*

Examples of the types of cases that might fall into the In Personam Exception include claims that seek a decree of specific performance of a contract of sale of foreign land (***Richard West and Partners (Inverness) Limited v Dick*** [1969] 2 Ch. 424 (CA)) and unjust enrichment actions to recover purchase monies in respect of foreign land (***Stevens v Hamed*** [2013] EWCA Civ 911). This might include recovery of deposits. Further claims may include one for the enforcement of security over foreign property (***Mercantile Investment Co v River Plate Co*** [1892] 2 Ch. 303).

However, if the *lex situs* (law of the land where the property is located) would prevent the enforcement of a particular decree or order, the Court may refuse to exercise its jurisdiction (see ***Luxe Holding Limited v Midland Resources Holding Limited*** [2010] EWHC 1908 (Ch) at [37]).

The Trusts and Estates Exception

The Trusts and Estates Exception is a further exception to the Moçambique Rule. If the question of title to, or the right to possession of, foreign immovable property has to be determined for the purpose of resolving a dispute in the administration of a deceased's estate or a trust that deals with a mix of foreign and domestic property, the Courts of England and Wales can determine the question. The rationale that sits behind this is that, if the Court is being asked to resolve a dispute in the administration of an estate or trust, if the incidental consequence is that it is necessary to determine title, or the rights to possession of, foreign land then it needs to be able to decide those issues to avoid a diversity of proceedings (see Griggs at [**70**]). There are a few supporting examples in case law where the Court has done just that:-

- The Court holding jurisdiction to decide who is entitled to land in Sardinia, Italy bequeathed by the testator upon trust alongside other property in England (***Re Piercy*** [1895] 1 Ch. 83).

- The Court holding jurisdiction to decide a dispute between a beneficiary of a will and a tenant in possession of Scottish land (the will also containing English property) (***Re Stirling*** [1908] 2 Ch. 344).

- The Court holding jurisdiction to determine entitlement to Italian property bequeathed under an Italian will (***Re Ross*** [1930] 1 Ch. 377).

- The Court holding jurisdiction, in a case where a testator produced English and Spanish wills, to determine to whom Spanish property bequeathed by the testator passed (***Re Duke of Wellington*** [1948] Ch. 118 (CA)).

The Torts Exception

As set out above, Section 30 (1) of the Civil Jurisdiction and Judgments Act 1982 confirms that the Courts of England and Wales (and Northern Ireland) hold jurisdiction to deal with proceedings for trespass to, or any other tort affecting, immovable property located abroad. However the Courts of England, Wales and Northern Ireland will not hold such jurisdiction if the proceedings are principally concerned with a question of the title to, or the right to possession of, the property in question. However, whilst outside the scope of this book, the reader should be aware that the Torts Exception is subject to the provisions of Schedule 4 of the Civil Jurisdiction and Judgments Act 1982 (see Section 30 (2)).

The question for the legal practitioner will be, when ascertaining if a particular action in tort should be brought in relation to foreign immovable property in the Courts of England and Wales, what is the meaning of '*principally concerned*' with a question of the title to, or the right to possession of, the property in question. In ***Re Polly Peck International Plc (In Administration)*** (No 2) [1998] 3 All ER 812, **829** (**"Re Polly Peck International"**) the Court of Appeal approved the lower Court's interpretation of the aforementioned phrase '*principally concerned*' which was interpreted in the following manner:-

> *"I consider that the purpose of s 30(1) of the 1982 Act is to preserve the Moçambique rule only in cases where the real issue in the proceedings is the question of title to, or the right to possession of, foreign land, and all other questions are merely incidental thereto."*

As can be seen from the above, in a tort related case, if and only if the real or main issue in the proceedings is the question of title or the right to possession of the foreign immovable property and all other issues are merely incidental or subordinate to that issue, the Moçambique Rule would capture the same. This is not a black and white question for the legal practitioner and each case will likely turn on its own facts and nuances in the framing of the claim. In ***The Bodo Community and Others v The Shell Petroleum Development Company of Nigeria Limited*** [2014] EWHC 1973 (TCC) ("**Bodo Community**"), a case involving a group claim for damages in light of oil spills in Nigeria, the High Court provided a useful set of examples at [**165**] to show the operation of Section 30 (1) of the Civil Jurisdiction and Judgments Act 1982:-

> *"(a) An individual claimant can readily show that he and his family for four generations before him have occupied and farmed land which he alleges was swamped by 50 cubic metres of oil from one of the spillages. Shell does not admit his connection to the land (simply putting him to proof) but runs a positive case that the oil spillage never reached this land. It might be said that the claim is not "principally" concerned with the title or possession to land.*
>
> *(b) An individual claimant alleges that he was a tenant of land right by the location of the pipe and which was swamped by 50 cubic metres of oil from one of the spillages and claims loss of use of the land. Shell admits that the land was so swamped by oil spilling from its pipe (and would in principle attract compensation) but runs a positive case that he was not ever a tenant. It might be said that his proceedings are "principally" concerned with the title or possession to land.*
>
> *(c) A chief, king or headman seeks in representative proceedings compensation but the only issue, on analysis is whether he is representative because he seeks to claim that he represents areas which are said to be outside his bailiwick. That might well be a claim which is "principally" concerned with the title or possession to land.*

> *(d) Representative proceedings are challenged on numerous grounds, for instance that many of those represented have no claim under the OPA as not having sufficient interests in the land, that they have suffered no "damage" which is recoverable under the Act, that many of those represented suffered no more than inconvenience etc and that the oil spillage did not reach where they lived. It might be said that the claim is not "principally" concerned with the title or possession to land, largely because there are a myriad of seriously contested issues.*
>
> *I am using the word "might" to avoid being prescriptive because the Court will need to look overall at claimants' claims and see if the issues are "principally" concerned with the title to or possession of land."*

As can be seen from the above, the Court is very careful to treat these are mere examples and caveats the examples by stating that the word "might" is being used to avoid being prescriptive. It is for the Court to assess the facts and the framing of each claim before it to determines whether the real issue is the title to, or the right to possession of, foreign immovable property and that all other issues in the proceedings, if any, are merely incidental to this question.

Further, one can see from the final example that even if the title to, or the right to possession of, foreign immovable property is a real issue in the case, if there are other equally seriously contested issues, the Torts Exception appears to be engaged. In other words, the title or right to possession issue cannot be the only real issue to which other issues are merely subordinate because in that situation the Moçambique Rule would be engaged instead.

In addition, the examples bring to light a particular procedural point. If a claim in tort is brought and it involves foreign immovable property, it is likely that the claimant's interests or rights in that property will be asserted by the claimant. However it is not at that point that the Court can really assess its jurisdiction (by reference to the Mozambique Rule and Section 30 (1) of the Civil Jurisdiction and Judgments Act 1982). It is only once the defence comes through that the Court will be in any position to really ascertain the existence of its jurisdiction. Indeed, the defence may put the claimant to proof on the issue of title, or right to possession, of the foreign immovable property (in which case this issue does not appear to amount to a principal issue in the case), admit the same (in which case this issue will not amount to a principal issue in the case), or make a positive case against the same (in which case this issue may amount to a principal issue in the case). The claim and the defence may bring to light a myriad of other prominent issues (thereby making the issue of title or rights to possession one of a number of real issues) or demonstrate that the only live and real issue is the title, or right to possession of, foreign immovable property (and thereby caught by the Mozambique Rule). Therefore at least in relation to a torts related case, it would appear the issue of jurisdiction will only be resolved post the filing of a defence.

The lesson for the legal practitioner is to examine the state of play on the pleadings and set out the list of issues, order them by prominence or importance and if the title to, or right to possession, of foreign immovable property is an issue in the case, examine if this is a real issue in the case and if so, whether the other issues are merely subordinate to it or are equally as important. It is important to take a step back and look at the overall picture of the case accordingly.

Summary of Key Practical and Tactical Tips

- For the legal practitioner the key question is not simply whether the dispute relates to immovable property located abroad but whether the Court is being asked to principally adjudicate on proprietary rights in rem as the real and only live issue in the case, or whether it is actually being asked to adjudicate upon personal obligations existing between the parties or otherwise equally important live issues in the case (or even the administration of estates and trusts). Simply because the case deals with foreign immovable property does not mean the Moçambique Rule is the end of the analysis.

- It is therefore of fundamental importance to analyse, assess and characterise the claim properly and correctly in order to determine the applicability of the jurisdictional principles at play when it comes to immovable property located abroad. This will determine if the Moçambique Rule applies or whether one or more of the exceptions to Moçambique Rule applies. This may be a strategic or tactical exercise particularly to avoid bringing proceedings abroad.

- The In Personam Exception is a broad exception involving personal obligations emanating from various fields of law (contract, equity, trusts and fraud). The Torts Exception stands or falls on the question of whether the claim is principally concerned with title to, or rights to possession of, foreign immovable property (i.e. whether it is the central issue with other issues, if any, being incidental to it). The Trusts and Estates Exception stands or falls on the question of whether, in reality, what is being asked of the Court is to decide a question in the administration of the trust or estate. This also exemplifies the importance of characterising the claim properly and correctly.

- When considering the In Personam Exception it is important to identify the source of the obligation early, ascertaining whether there is a contract, a fiduciary relationship or an alleged fraud or other unconscionable conduct to be reversed.

- Even where jurisdiction is said to exist, the Court may refuse to exercise jurisdiction by way of its discretion where foreign law prevents enforcement. This is something to bear in mind.

- When it comes to the Torts Exception in particular it may be important to analyse all the pleadings to ascertain the real issues between the parties to see if the exception is engaged. It may be that it is only at this point the Court can determine the existence of jurisdiction. Jurisdictional issues in this respect will likely crystallise after the filing and service of the defence when title may be admitted or put to proof or positively contested for example.

- A practical approach that may be taken is to identify all the issues from the pleadings, assess their relative importance and determine if the question of title to, or rights to possession of, foreign immovable property is the dominant issue or not.

- The special jurisdictional principles considered in this Chapter and the previous Chapter emphasise a particular important practical point: the need to take a step back and assess the overall picture of the case in a holistic way as early as possible.

CHAPTER FIVE

THE FURTHER REQUIREMENTS OF JURISDICTION: SERVICE AND CHALLENGE

In Chapter Two the point was made that it is important to understand the meaning of jurisdiction as the power of the Court to compel a party to be brought before it to try a case. A further point was made that there are two questions which stem from this meaning of jurisdiction, namely whether the Court's jurisdiction exists and whether the Court's jurisdiction should be exercised.

Chapters Three and Four set out the special jurisdictional rules and principles that apply to cases involving foreign immovable property (dealing with the existence of jurisdiction question). Those special jurisdictional rules and principles ought to be considered first when examining such a case. However the general rules and requirements cannot be forgotten and these rules and requirements stem from the rules of service in CPR Part 6 and the rules relating to the challenge of jurisdiction in CPR Part 11.

For the purposes of this Chapter it is important to remember the definition of jurisdiction contained in the CPR as it relates to physical jurisdiction. CPR r 2.3 confirms that jurisdiction means, unless the context requires otherwise, England and Wales and any part of the territorial waters of the United Kingdom adjoining England and Wales.

This Chapter provides an outline of the key rules and principles only and the reader is directed to CPR Part 6 and CPR Part 11 and the key commentary contained in the White Book 2026, Volume 1 and any updates to the same.

Service within the Jurisdiction of England and Wales

As set out in Chapter Two, outside the special jurisdictional rules and principles relating to foreign immovable property discussed in Chapters Three and Four, in order to establish the existence of the Court's jurisdiction to a dispute, proceedings have to be effectively and validly served on the defendant. In a case where the defendant is located in England and Wales valid and effective service of proceedings in accordance with Part II and Practice Direction 6A of CPR Part 6 will otherwise establish the Court's jurisdiction in relation to the dispute. Either the defendant will accept service of the proceedings or will dispute jurisdiction under CPR Part 11.

Service outside the Jurisdiction of England and Wales

Section IV of CPR Part 6 deals with the service of the claim form and other documents outside the jurisdiction. CPR r 6.36 confirms that in any proceedings to which CPR r 6.32 or 6.33 does not apply, the claimant may serve a claim form out of the jurisdiction with the permission of the Court if any of the grounds set out in paragraph 3.1 of Practice Direction 6B CPR apply. Therefore in these circumstances, service of proceedings outside the jurisdiction of England and Wales requires the Court's permission. Therefore this general requirement of service to establish the existence of jurisdiction (and as will be shown, the exercise of jurisdiction) requires the permission of the Court where service is to be effected abroad. When dealing with foreign immovable property, there is a good chance the defendant is located abroad.

Under r 6.37 (1) CPR an application for permission under r 6.36 CPR must set out (a) which ground in paragraph 3.1 of Practice Direction 6B CPR is relied upon, (b) that the claimant believes that the claim has a reasonable prospect of success and (c) the defendant's address or, if not known, in what place the defendant is, or is likely, to be found. Further, and importantly, under r 6.36 (3) CPR the Court will not give permission unless satisfied that England and Wales is the proper place in which to bring the claim (i.e. *forum conveniens*). This latter point shows that, when it comes to the service of proceedings outside of the jurisdiction of England and Wales, the Court needs to be satisfied about both the existence and the exercise of jurisdiction.

Based on the above, when considering to seek the Court's permission for the service of proceedings outside of the jurisdiction, there are four elements to the test to establish the Court's existence and exercise of jurisdiction (see the outline of the test in ***Altimo Holdings v Kyrgyz Mobil Tel Ltd*** [2011] UKPC 7 at [71] ("**Altimo**") as set out below):-

- The existence of a good arguable case against a foreign defendant that the claim falls under one of more of the gateways under paragraph 3.1 of Practice Direction 6B CPR.

The reader is directed to paragraph 3.1 of Practice Direction 6B CPR which sets out the various 'service out' gateways under which a claimant's case would need to fall in order to obtain the Court's permission to serve proceedings out of the jurisdiction. In the context of the exceptions to the Moçambique Rule, the applicable gateways are likely to be in respect of claims in relation to contracts (paragraph 3.1 (6)-(8A)), claims in tort (paragraph 3.1 (9)), trust related claims (paragraph 3.1 (12) to (13), (15)) and unjust enrichment actions (paragraph 3.1 (16)). The reader is directed, if and when making an application for permission to serve outside the jurisdiction, to the details contained in paragraph 3.1 of Practice Direction 6B CPR and the supporting 'Notes on Heads of Jurisdiction in Paragraph 3.1 of

Practice Direction 6B' contained in the White Book, Volume 1, 2026 and any updates to the same. The aim of the gateways is to find "*substantial and not merely casual or adventitious link between the cause of action and England*" (***Brownlie v Four Season Holdings Inc*** [2017] UKSC 80 at [**28**] ("**Brownlie**")). The ground(s) relied upon must be set out in the application for permission to serve out of the jurisdiction. The burden of proof is on the claimant.

No doubt the reader will notice that paragraph 3.1 (11) of Practice Direction 6B CPR provides for a gateway where the subject matter of the claim relates wholly or principally to property within the jurisdiction, provided that nothing under this paragraph shall render justiciable the title to or the right to possession of immovable property outside England and Wales. This gateway is an express reference to the Moçambique Rule.

A good arguable case, when dealing with issues of fact, is a reference to a standard which is higher than a serious issue to be tried or a real prospect of success but lower than a balance of probabilities (see ***Carvill America Incorporated and Others v Camperdown UK Limited and Others*** [2005] EWCA Civ 645 at [**45**]). A gloss was added to this test in ***Canada Trust v Stolzenberg*** [1998] 1 W.L.R. 547, **555** where the Court equated a good arguable case with one side having a much better argument on the material available. This gloss was further explained and expanded in Brownlie in the following manner (at [7]):-

> *"What is meant is (i) that the claimant must supply a plausible evidential basis for the application of a relevant jurisdictional gateway; (ii) that if there is an issue of fact about it, or some other reason for doubting whether it applies, the Court must take a view on the material available if it can reliably do so; but (iii) the nature of the issue and the limitations of the material available at the interlocutory stage may be such that no reliable assessment can be made, in which case there is a good arguable case for the application*

of the gateway if there is a plausible (albeit contested) evidential basis for it. I do not believe that anything is gained by the word "much", which suggests a superior standard of conviction that is both uncertain and unwarranted in this context."

However, it may be that the existence of a gateway (and therefore the existence of jurisdiction) turns, not on issues of fact, but a question or argument of law and construction. If the facts are clear, the Court is likely to decide the question or argument of law or construction rather than seeing if there is a good arguable case on that question or argument of law or construction. See, for example, ***Chellaram v Chellaram (No. 2)*** [2002] EWHC 632 (Ch) at [**136**] where the Court explained that if jurisdiction depended on determining the applicable law of a contract, the Court would decide it rather than apply the good arguable case test. Therefore if the existence of jurisdiction depended on identifying the applicable law, the claimant would have to satisfy the Court of the applicable law. The good arguable case test would however apply if there was a factual issue involved.

In ***Lungowe and Others v Vedanta Resources Plc and Others*** [2017] EWCA Civ 1528 at [**63**], the Court expanded on this and stated the following when considering the test as it relates to points or arguments of law:-

"In my judgment, this analysis leads to the following conclusions. (1) In general, a real issue between the relevant parties is to be equated with a properly arguable case or serious question to be tried. (2) Where the argument or question goes to the existence of the jurisdiction, it should be decided if the facts are clear. (3) However, if the facts are not clear or the point of law is exceptionally difficult and doubtful, the test should remain that set out in (1) above. (4) This leaves open the question of the extent to which the facts are clear, and what amounts to 'exceptionally difficult and doubtful' points of law. As to the former point...the Court should proceed on

> *the basis of a pleaded case. So far as the latter point is concerned, it might be thought that the more doubtful the point of law, the more cautious the Court should be, since the question of law goes to the existence of the jurisdiction."*

The above demonstrates that if the facts are clear on the pleadings, the Court will decide the point of law rather than reverting to the good arguable case threshold. However if the facts are not clear or the point of law is an exceptionally difficult or doubtful one, the Court will apply the good arguable case threshold instead. The more doubtful the point of law, the more cautious the Court will be given the question of law goes to the existence of jurisdiction.

- The existence of a serious issue to be tried on the merits of the claim.

The claim must hold real, as opposed to fanciful prospects of success (the same test as that applied to summary judgment applications – see Altimo at [**71**]). The burden of proof is on the claimant.

- Whether England and Wales is the proper place in which to bring the claim (i.e. *forum conveniens*).

As briefly touched upon in Chapter Two, even if service of proceedings can be validly effected abroad because the claim has real prospects of success and there is a good arguable case on one or more of the jurisdictional gateways, the Court will still need to be satisfied that England and Wales is the proper place in which to bring the claim (i.e. England and Wales is the proper forum – *forum conveniens*).

The key case dealing with this aspect of the test is ***Spiliada Maritime Corporation v Cansulex Ltd*** [1987] A.C. 460 ("**the Spiliada**"). The reader is directed to **478E to 482A** of the Spiliada. Those paragraphs confirm the following points. The burden of proof is on the claimant to satisfy the Court that England and Wales is clearly and distinctly the appropriate forum for the trial of the action. There are a number of non-exhaustive connecting factors to take into account. This may be the residence or place of business of the defendant (the foreign entity), the relevant ground or gateway being invoked, the applicable law in relation to the dispute, where a contract was made, the nature of the dispute, the legal and practical issues involved, the local knowledge, the location and availability of witnesses and their evidence and expense. Further a question may arise as to whether justice can be obtained in an alternative forum, or only obtained with excessive cost, delay or inconvenience. The aim is to identify the forum in which the case can be suitably tried for the interests of all the parties and for the ends of justice. The weight to be attached to the non-exhaustive factors, in all the circumstances, is that which the Court considers to be appropriate. Each case turns on its own facts and first instance authorities are mere illustrations and examples (***Jong v HSBC Private Bank (Monoco) SA*** [2015] EWCA Civ 1057 at [**18**] referring to Millett LJ in ***Jaggard v Sawyer*** [1995] 1 WLR 269, **288**). However, the location of witnesses and documentation may not be as an important factor in the modern day and age in light of technological advancements (e.g. video links and electronic disclosure) – see ***Ditto Ltd v Drive-Thru Records LLC*** [2021] EWHC 2035 (Ch) at [**83**] and ***Al Mana Lifestyle Trading LLC v United Fidelity Insurance Co PSC*** [2022] EWHC 2049 (Comm) at [**98**].

- Whether the Court ought to grant permission to serve out of the jurisdiction in exercise of its ultimate discretion.

Even if the Court is satisfied with regards to the gateways, the merits of the claim and England and Wales as being the appropriate forum, it holds an ultimate discretion to grant or refuse service out of proceedings (and therefore the existence and exercise of jurisdiction). It is unclear in what circumstances this general discretion will be exercised albeit in ***Schothorst and Schuitema v Franz Dauter GmbH***

[1973] 2 Lloyd's Rep. 91 it appears factors such as the lengthy delay in seeking permission to serve and likelihood of a limitation defence may be factors pointing in the direction of refusing permission to serve or leading to setting aside of orders for permission to serve. Indeed the attempt to seek permission for service out of the jurisdiction to effectively extend the four month validity of the claim form which had expired to six months failed in ***National Bank of Greece SA v Outhwaite*** [2001] C.P. Rep.69 (see [**46**]). The Court stated at [**50**] that *"the power of the Courts to permit service out of the jurisdiction should not be exercised to save the Claimants from the consequences of not issuing and serving proceedings more promptly."* In ***Erste Group AF (London) v JSC (VMZ Red October)*** [2015] EWCA Civ 379 (at [**150**]) the Court stated that, in exercise of the ultimate discretion, consideration ought to have been given to the commercial drivers behind the claimant's issue of proceedings (in this case the commercial driver to issue against the first and second defendants was to enable a claim to be brought against the third and fifth defendants and to attempt to execute against their assets). This, again, may be a factor for the Court to take into account more generally when exercising its ultimate discretion albeit, given the above, it appears each case will turn on its own facts and considerations.

For completeness and to explain the practicality, a claimant would need to make a without notice N244 application for permission to serve out in accordance with CPR Part 23 supported by a witness statement. Further, CPR r 6.37 (5) confirms that where the Court gives permission to serve a claim form out of the jurisdiction it will specify the periods within which the defendant may file an acknowledgment of service, file or serve an admission, file a defence or file any other response or document required by a rule in another Part, any other enactment or a practice direction and may give directions about the method of service. The reader is directed to paragraph 6.2 to 6.4, 6.6 and the Table contained in Practice Direction 6B CPR.

The Defendant's Dispute of Jurisdiction: CPR Part 11

Part 11 CPR deals with the procedure available to a foreign defendant, or indeed any defendant, to dispute the Court's jurisdiction following the service of proceedings. Under CPR r 11.1 (1) a defendant who wishes to dispute the Court's jurisdiction to try the claim (i.e. the existence of jurisdiction) or argue that the Court should not exercise its jurisdiction (i.e. the exercise of jurisdiction), may apply to the Court for an order declaring that it has no such jurisdiction or should not exercise any jurisdiction which it may have. Under CPR r 11.1 (2), a defendant who wishes to make such an application must first file an acknowledgment of service and his application contesting jurisdiction must, under CPR r 11.1 (4), be made within 14 days of filing an acknowledgment of service and be supported by evidence. If the Court declares it has no jurisdiction or will not exercise jurisdiction, it may (under CPR r 11.1 (6)), *inter alia*, set aside the claim form, the service of the claim form and/or stay the proceedings.

The crux of the above, for the purposes of this book, is that if a defendant challenges the order granting permission to serve outside the jurisdiction, the defendant may seek an order by way of an application under CPR Part 11 to set aside the permission order and set aside service of the claim form. This may be, for example, on the grounds that service was not validly effected or England and Wales is not clearly the appropriate forum for the trial of action. This will therefore either be a challenge to the existence of jurisdiction or the exercise of jurisdiction.

However, if service was validly effected within the jurisdiction, the defendant may make an application under CPR Part 11 to seek an order to stay the proceedings on the grounds of *forum non conveniens* (i.e. England and Wales is not clearly the appropriate forum for the trial of the action). The burden of demonstrating the same rests on the defendant. This is a challenge to the exercise of jurisdiction. The reader's attention is drawn to the Spiliada at 475C to 478E where the Court discussed the principles applicable to the defendant's seeking of a stay in these circumstances. In summary:-

- A stay will only be granted on the grounds of *forum non conveniens* where the Court is satisfied that there is some other available forum, having competent jurisdiction, which is the appropriate forum for the trial of action (i.e. in which the case may be tried more suitably for the interests of all the parties and the ends of justice). The defendant must show that England is not the natural or appropriate forum for the trial and that there is another available forum which is clearly or distinctly more appropriate than England and Wales. The natural forum is that with which the action has the most real and substantial connection.

- In general the burden of proof rests on the defendant to persuade the Court to exercise its discretion to grant a stay. If the Court is satisfied that there is another available forum which is *prima facie* the appropriate forum for the trial of the action the burden will switch to the claimant to show there are special circumstances by reason of which justice requires that the trial should nevertheless take place in England and Wales.

- Factors to consider will be the same or similar to the factors relating to *forum conveniens* and will also include the connection of the defendant to the England and Wales forum (and the strength of the same), whether justice can be done in the other forum at substantially less inconvenience or expense (e.g. availability of witnesses and documents), the law governing the dispute or transaction, residence and location.

- The aforementioned special circumstances include all the circumstances of the case (and beyond the aforementioned connecting factors). This may include the fact that the claimant will not obtain justice in the foreign jurisdiction. The burden of proof is on the claimant in this respect.

Summary of Key Practical and Tactical Tips

- Chapters Three and Four examined the specific rules of jurisdiction that applies to cases involving foreign immovable property. This Chapter provides for the general additional rules of jurisdiction that must also be considered by the Court which is tied to the procedural rules of service of proceedings and challenges to jurisdiction. The general and specific rules work hand in hand to establish both the existence and exercise of jurisdiction when dealing with a case involving foreign immovable property.

- CPR Part 6 and CPR Part 11 provides for the procedural frameworks to establish the existence and exercise of jurisdiction and challenge the existence and exercise of jurisdiction respectively. For example, if a defendant validly served with proceedings within the jurisdiction sought to challenge the existence of jurisdiction by invoking the Moçambique Rule, he would need to make an application under CPR Part 11.

- When examining the issue of jurisdiction, one can start by examining the application of the Moçambique Rule and the exceptions to it before turning to the general additional principles of jurisdiction. However, when considering the general additional principles of jurisdiction, one can start by asking whether the defendant can be served within the jurisdiction or is required to be served outside the jurisdiction. If the defendant is required to be served outside the jurisdiction, the practitioner will need to make an application for permission to serve outside the jurisdiction and satisfy the Court of the four part service out test: is there a good arguable case in relation to one of more of the gateways for service out contained in paragraph 3 of Practice Direction 6B CPR, is there a serious issue to be tried on the merits, is England and Wales clearly and distinctly the most appropriate forum for the trial of the action and are there any other considerations for the Court in the exercise of its ultimate discretion in granting or refusing permission to serve out.

- It must be remembered that the ability to validly effect service of proceedings is not the sole answer to the issue of jurisdiction but part of the answer – the Moçambique Rule, the exceptions and the question of *forum conveniens* or *forum non conveniens* are critical in analysing jurisdiction too.

- The gateways in paragraph 3.1 of Practice Direction 6B CPR are the foundation for examining service out of the jurisdiction. It is important to pick the most suitable and accurate gateways based on the nature of the case. This is important when examining the exceptions to the Moçambique Rule. The characterisation of the claim should align with the gateway being applied to it.

- It is important for a claimant to be thoroughly prepared by anticipating if an application for service out of the jurisdiction is going to be required to be made. The facts must be properly and clearly pleaded in the Particulars of Claim and, ideally, a clear evidential basis ought to exist to make out the good arguable case and real prospects of success thresholds as well as demonstrating *forum conveniens*. If the issue of jurisdiction rests purely on a point of law (e.g. the applicable law of a contract) expect the Court to deal with it from the outset. It is important therefore to be fully prepared with the answer to the point of law in the client's favour.

- The issue of *forum conveniens* or, if the defendant intends to challenge the exercise of jurisdiction and apply for a stay, *forum non conveniens*, is likely to be a central battlefield when considering the general additional principles of jurisdiction. When it comes to foreign immovable property, irrespective of the applicability of an exception to the Moçambique Rule, the Court may place emphasis on the location of the property and the *lex situs*. If deciding on *forum conveniens*, a claimant will need to establish and argue connecting factors to England and Wales as clearly and distinctly the appropriate forum in which to try the action. If deciding on *forum non conveniens*, it will be for the defendant to establish that another forum is clearly and distinctly the appropriate forum in which to try the action.

- The legal practitioner must understand the swinging burden of proof. In cases where service is validly effected in the jurisdiction, it will be for the defendant to challenge the existence or exercise of jurisdiction. If the defendant alleges *forum non conveniens*, it will be for him to satisfy the Court that an alternative forum is clearly and distinctly appropriate for the trial of the action and that a stay of proceedings is appropriate. The burden will shift to the claimant where, *prima facie*, there is an alternative more appropriate forum, to establish special circumstances that the trial of the action ought to still take place in England and Wales. In cases where permission to serve outside the jurisdiction is sought, it will be for the claimant to satisfy the Court that England and Wales is clearly and distinctly the appropriate forum for the trial of the action.

- It is important to act promptly when seeking permission to serve out to avoid the Court exercising its ultimate discretion in refusing permission. It is best to stay on top of the procedural requirements. It is unlikely that the Court will permit service out as a workaround from the claimant's failure to serve proceedings on time within the jurisdiction.

- If acting for the defendant seeking to challenge jurisdiction, it is important to comply with the procedural requirements in CPR Part 11 in a prompt fashion particularly to avoid the consequence of being deemed to have submitted to the jurisdiction. It is important to clarify what the defendant's argument is – is it a challenge to the existence of jurisdiction or the exercise of jurisdiction? This will help understand the answer to the next question which is what relief the defendant is seeking – is it a stay of proceedings or the set aside of the permission order, the claim form or service of proceedings for example.

- As Chapters Two to Five have demonstrated, the issue of jurisdiction is a dynamic and moving one. Whilst it is important to analyse and iron out the issue of jurisdiction early in the proceedings, whether acting for the claimant or defendant, it is important to keep a keen eye on the jurisdiction question as proceedings progress (e.g. the Torts Exception highlights that, until the defence is received, it may not yet be clear whether the Torts Exception applies).

- It is important for the practitioner to assess the question of jurisdiction tactically and commercially – what advantage or disadvantage does the conduct of proceedings in England and Wales, or an alternative forum, really bring? Are there enforcement advantages? Are arguments over jurisdiction worth the fight?

CHAPTER SIX

APPLICABLE LAW: CONTRACTS RELATED TO FOREIGN IMMOVABLE PROPERTY

Chapter Four, *inter alia*, explored the In Personam Exception to the Moçambique Rule in the context of analysing the existence of the jurisdiction of the Courts of England and Wales when a dispute involves foreign immovable property. By way of the In Personam Exception, the Courts of England and Wales have jurisdiction to entertain proceedings that deal with personal contractual obligations between the parties (e.g. specific performance of a contract of sale) (subject, of course, to the application of the general rules and principles of jurisdiction as set out in Chapter Five). In reality, such proceedings do not directly deal with proprietary in rem rights in the foreign property itself, albeit indirectly the outcome of such proceedings could have an influence on such proprietary in rem rights in the foreign property.

This Chapter examines the next branch in analysing a conflict of laws dilemma, namely the applicable law in relation to the dispute. More specifically, this Chapter examines the applicable law relating to contracts dealing with foreign immovable property (particularly dealing with proprietary rights in rem) following a Court's conclusion that it has jurisdiction to deal with the matter.

In order to determine the applicable law of the contract, the legal practitioner would need to consider and consult Regulation (EC) No 593/2008 of the European Parliament and of the Council of 17 June

2008 on the law applicable to contractual obligations (Rome I) (Retained EU Legislation) ("**UK Rome I Regulations**"). The reader is directed to the detail of the UK Rome I Regulations and associated commentary for further detail. The below is provided in outline only:-

- The parties may have chosen the applicable law in accordance with Article 3 of the UK Rome I Regulations in which case that law applies to the contract dealing with the foreign immovable property (particularly dealing with the proprietary rights in rem).

- If the parties have not chosen the applicable law as above, a contract dealing with proprietary rights in rem in foreign immovable property is governed by the *lex situs* (i.e. the law of the country where the foreign property is seated). Article 4 (1) (c) of the UK Rome I Regulations states that a contract relating to a right in rem in immovable property shall be governed by the law of the country where the property is situated.

- However, there is an escape clause to the *lex situs*. By way of Article 4 (3) of the UK Rome I Regulations, where it is clear from all the circumstances of the case that the contract is manifestly more closely connected with a country other than that indicated directly above, the law of that other country shall apply instead.

The UK Rome I Regulations covers the determination of the law that applies to contractual obligations and it does not cover proprietary rights. Therefore the aforementioned rules do not apply to the transfer and conveyance of proprietary interests themselves but only the underlying contractual arrangements in this respect (e.g. a contract of sale or transfer).

The general rule when a contract is entered into between parties relating to rights in rem in foreign immovable property is that the law is governed by the country where the property is seated. However the escape clause provides for a high threshold test to displace the *lex situs* as the applicable law where it is clear from all the circumstances of the case that the contract is manifestly more closely connected with a country other than the *lex situs*. In those circumstances the law of the other country will apply instead. The Court can look at all the circumstances of the case to decide the applicability of the escape clause and so in this respect there may be an infinite number of connecting factors to a different country than the *lex situs*. However, the reference to the need to show *clearly* a *manifestly* more closely connected country demonstrates the high hurdle that needs to be crossed, through the use of the connecting factors, to displace the *lex situs* as the applicable law of the contract.

The escape clause could, arguably, be successfully utilised where the contract is altogether connected with one country (e.g. location of the parties or where the contract was executed and to be performed) and the only foreign element is the foreign immovable property. This was the opinion of Advocate General Bot in ***Intercontainer Interfrigo SC (ICF) v Balkenende Oosthuizen BV*** [2010] Q.B. 411 at [78]. However this was merely an opinion. There is also the argument that the location of the immovable property is a strong connecting factor and simply asserting that the contract is altogether connected with one country aside from the foreign immovable property may not be enough and something more may be required to displace the *lex situs* as the governing law. For example, a displacing connecting factor may be that the contract in question has a very close relationship with another contract or contracts (see Recital 20 of the UK Rome I Regulations).

Further, it is important to bear in mind the link between the principles of jurisdiction and applicable law in this context. As mentioned in

Chapter Four, the Court is unlikely to entertain jurisdiction even if the In Personam Exception is engaged if the *lex situs* would prevent the enforcement of a particular order or decree (e.g. not recognise the title of the buyer). Indeed, for example, when it comes to specific performance, equity will not act in vain in these circumstances. The Court would simply refuse to grant the remedy. The reader is also directed to Articles 9 (3) and 12 (2) of the UK Rome I Regulations. The former states that effect may be given to the overriding mandatory provisions of the law of the country where the obligations arising out of the contract have to be or have been performed, in so far as those overriding mandatory provisions render the performance of the contract unlawful. The latter states that, in relation to the manner of performance and the steps to be taken in the event of defective performance, regard shall be had to the law of the country in which performance takes place.

All of the above demonstrates that the branches of jurisdiction and applicable law, whilst considered separately in any analysis, can and do overlap. In relation to applicable law, the UK Rome I Regulations deals squarely with contractual obligations that relate to rights in rem in respect of foreign immovable property. In relation to jurisdiction, the In Personam Exception deals squarely with personal obligations that relate to rights in rem in respect of foreign immovable property. Neither deals with the question of the title to, or rights to possession of, foreign immovable property. The only difference is that whilst the In Personam Exception provides a stepping stone towards establishing the existence of the jurisdiction of the Courts of England and Wales, the general rule when it comes to applicable law is that the applicable law of the *lex situs* will apply. Ordinarily in these circumstances the Courts of England and Wales would be applying foreign law unless displaced by the escape clause. These are points to anticipate when dealing with *forum conveniens* or *forum non conveniens* because it may be that because foreign law is to apply to the dispute, the Court refuses to exercise its jurisdiction holding that the clear and appropriate forum is that of the *lex situs.*

Summary of Key Practical and Tactical Tips

- In order to determine the applicable law of a contract related to rights in rem in foreign immovable property, one must make sure to distinguish between contractual obligations and proprietary rights. UK Rome I Regulations govern underlying contractual obligations and not the transfer of proprietary rights themselves.

- In terms of understanding what the applicable law is, one must start with the question of whether the parties have chosen the governing law under Article 3 of the UK Rome I Regulations. If so, that will determine the matter. In the absence of choice, the default rule is that the *lex situs* is the applicable law of a contract dealing with rights in rem of foreign immovable property.

- However, it may be that the escape clause could be utilised if another country is manifestly more closely connected to the contract in question. However the escape clause is an exceptional clause with a high threshold test. It will not easily apply and will depend on the exceptional circumstances of the case. It is important to identify and assess the connecting factors (e.g. the location of parties, place of performance, existence of related contracts) and weigh these against the strong connecting factor that is the *lex situs* – the location of the physical seat of the property.

- It is important to remember that jurisdiction and applicable law, whilst separate branches in any analysis, do converge. If foreign law applies this may support a forum challenge by a defendant (*forum non conveniens)* or influence the Court's view when it comes to determining *forum conveniens* as part of the test for service of proceedings out of the jurisdiction.

- Enforceability is clearly of importance both at the jurisdiction and applicable law stage. A Court may refuse jurisdiction if its decrees or orders cannot be enforced in the foreign jurisdiction due to the law of that country. Equally if the law of the country prohibits the enforcement of such an order or decree (e.g. the overriding mandatory provisions of the law of the place of performance and the law of the country where the performance takes place with respect to the manner of performance and steps to be taken in the event of defective performance), the Court is not going to grant the relief sought in any event.

CHAPTER SEVEN

APPLICABLE LAW: TRANSFERS OF FOREIGN IMMOVABLE PROPERTY RIGHTS

The previous Chapter examined the position on applicable law that relates to the underlying contractual arrangements related to rights in rem in foreign immovable property. This brief Chapter examines the position on applicable law as it relates to inter vivos transfers of rights in rem in foreign immovable property by way of comparison.

Unsurprisingly, proprietary rights in relation to foreign immovable property are governed by the *lex situs* (i.e. the law of the country where the property is physically seated) – see ***Re Anziani*** [1930] 1 Ch. 407, 424. This fits in neatly with the Moçambique Rule. Any questions relating to proprietary rights over foreign immovable property are governed by the law where the property is situated. Therefore if the Courts of England and Wales are required, in what appears to be the unlikely event given the content of the previous Chapters, to determine any proprietary rights over foreign immovable property it would have to follow the *lex situs*.

Of course, as examined in the previous Chapters, the Courts of England and Wales could take jurisdiction under the In Personam Exception, apply English law, and enter a judgment requiring the specific performance of a contract of sale by way of the execution of a transfer of foreign immovable property. This is the indirect effect of the In Personam Exception and the rules of applicable law as it relates to contracts involving rights in rem in relation to foreign immovable property.

Accordingly, whilst contractual arrangements may be governed by different laws, the transfer of foreign immovable property itself (i.e. proprietary rights in rem) are exclusively governed by the *lex situs*.

Summary of Key Practical and Tactical Tips

- Always distinguish between the transfer of foreign immovable property interests and the underlying contractual arrangements. The former is governed by the *lex situs* and the contract may be governed by an entirely separate law.

- It is important to use the In Personam Exception to jurisdiction with care and thought. An English Court may order a party to act and execute a transfer of foreign immovable property but the effectiveness of such an order depends on the *lex situs*. This touches on the consideration of the effectiveness of enforcement. If the transfer would prove ineffective for example, the Court may refuse to make the order in the first place.

- In any case involving proprietary rights in rem in relation to foreign immovable property, it is important to undertake thorough research into the laws of the location where the property is situated. There is likely to be different rules on registration, transfers and legal and equitable interests (if equity is a recognised concept) for example.

- As a side point, if one is undertaking the drafting of a contract involving foreign immovable property and transfers of foreign property interests, it is important to anticipate and understand the requirements of the *lex situs* and whether a transfer would be legally effective abroad. This will likely save a lot of hassle in the event of a dispute.

- Even if the relief is framed in personam, one ought to question whether the relief would actually determine proprietary rights in relation to the foreign property and whether this risks the Courts considering the *lex situs* to apply to the dispute (and the consequences of the same).

- It might be appropriate to obtain expert advice on the foreign law to ensure that, if the *lex situs* is to apply in any way, shape or form, this will not present a sticking point for the client in the litigation. This might be a worthwhile step to take pre-action to save time and cost in the event litigation is not warranted by the end of the analysis.

CHAPTER EIGHT

PLEADING AND PROVING FOREIGN LAW

In disputes involving foreign immovable property, cementing of jurisdiction and the identification of the applicable law is not enough. The next challenge lies in making sure the case is presented well and proved to the satisfaction of the Court in the client's best interests.

Once the legal practitioner is satisfied that England and Wales is the correct and most appropriate jurisdiction in relation to the dispute concerning foreign immovable property and is also satisfied that the applicable law in relation to the said dispute is a foreign law, the next question is how the case is to be best presented to the Court. This is a question of pleading and proving foreign law. This is a brief Chapter providing an outline on the topic and the reader is urged to consult major practitioner texts in this area for further details.

Firstly, and generally speaking, if a party is going to rely on foreign law it must be pleaded and proved as a fact. Therefore the particulars of the foreign law must be set out in the particulars of claim (or, as appropriate, in the defence). The foreign law must be proved through the use of evidence:-

- The evidence may consist of the expert opinion of judges, former judges, lawyers, former lawyers and academic lawyers from the foreign jurisdiction.

- The experts may refer to sources of foreign law such as foreign statutes and foreign decisions, and so this is another form of documentary evidence.

- The sources of foreign law ought to be supplemented by evidence of how to interpret the said sources of foreign law.

- Subject to the provisions of Section 4 of the Civil Evidence Act 1972 to which the reader is directed, previous English decisions on foreign law may be admissible in evidence to prove foreign law.

It is important to note that the Courts will still use its own critical thinking in examining the expert opinions as it would do in any other case involving expert evidence. It does not need to accept the expert opinion outright. The weight to be placed on the expert opinion and documentary evidence in support is up to the Court. It is also important to note that the burden of proving foreign law rests on the party relying upon it.

However, it is not necessary for a party to rely on foreign law. A party is not obliged to do so. However, there are certain consequences in not doing so in a case where there is foreign immovable property involved (or indeed any foreign aspect to the case) and foreign law therefore might have been applicable. The consequences are discussed by Lord Leggatt in ***Brownlie v FS Cairo (Nile Plaza) LLC*** [2021] UKSC 45 ("**Brownlie II**"):-

- The default rule is that, where foreign law is not pleaded, the Court applies English law in its own right ([**112**]).

- In cases where foreign law is recognised to apply but it has not been proven, it is presumed that the foreign law is the same as the domestic law ([**119**]). The question is one of fact – in the circumstances is it reasonable to expect that the applicable foreign law is likely to be materially similar to English law on the matter in issue ([**126**]). The presumption is a rule of evidence concerned with what the content of the foreign law should be taken to be ([112]). The reader is directed to the justification of the rule at [123-125] of Brownlie II. Guidance on the application of this presumption of similarity can be found at [143-149] of Brownlie II.

When it comes to the aforementioned consequences it must be remembered that the decision to plead and/or prove foreign law may be a tactical or commercial one. It is up to the parties to decide on whether foreign law is to be pleaded and evidence adduced of the same in support of their cases. It may be that foreign law does not need to be relied upon as the content of the law is the same as English law. Further, whilst the Court may rely solely on foreign legal sources (see [143-149] in Brownlie II), it is likely that potentially costly foreign expert evidence will be required (which may also be time consuming to obtain given the need to communicate with a foreign expert who may be situated in another jurisdiction). Alternatively, the party will have to consider if the risk of relying upon the default rule or presumption of similarity is a risk worth taking. As explained at [143-149] in Brownlie II, this might be a risk that can be taken early on in proceedings during the pleadings phase, but one can question if this is a risk worth taking at trial stage. By trial stage it would appear more appropriate to get the client's house in order and not rely on defaults or presumptions but clear and cogent evidence of foreign law.

Summary of Key Practical and Tactical Tips

- It is important to identify early if foreign law needs to be pleaded and proved. In cases involving foreign immovable property, as described in the last couple of Chapters, it may be that the *lex situs* governs the applicable law.

- If pleading foreign law (which is treated as a fact), it is important to ensure that the particulars of those facts are pleaded thoroughly, specifically, clearly and accurately.

- In cases involving foreign immovable property, it is likely expert opinion will be needed to prove foreign law given the technicalities involved in the subject. The cost involved in instructing foreign lawyers or judges to give this evidence is something to take account of plus the timing of the receipt of the expert report. It is important to ensure any expert evidence adds value to the case.

- It is also important to choose the expert carefully based on expertise and experience in giving foreign expert evidence with clarity. One should assess if the expert is capable of expressing foreign legal concepts with simplicity and by cross-referencing and comparing English law. An initial discussion with the expert along with consideration of their CV will be important in this respect.

- One must ensure the expert provides supporting documentary evidence by way of foreign legal sources (statutes and foreign decisions) to strengthen his opinion. However it must be remembered that blind reliance should not be placed on the expert's opinion. The Court will undertake its own critical analysis of that evidence and indeed the other side may proffer their own expert evidence. One must treat the expert evidence as one would any other expert evidence in analysis and evaluation, providing questions to the expert to clarify and stress testing his opinion where necessary.

- One must keep in mind the consequences of not pleading and proving foreign law by way of the default rule and the presumption of similarity. It is important to question if the use of English law will suffice (e.g. because it is materially the same as the foreign law) or whether the case is one where foreign law must be pleaded and proved to make out the client's case for relief.

- What may appear acceptable at the pleading stage by reliance on the default rule or presumption of similarity may not be suitable at trial. It is important to stay vigilant on whether foreign law needs to be pleaded and proved during the life of the litigation and action taken, if so decided, as early as possible (e.g. applications to amend pleadings to prove foreign law).

- The foreign law ought to align with, and support, the case on jurisdiction. It should support the framing of the claim and any exception to the Moçambique Rule relied on.

- If a clear decision is made to plead and prove foreign law, it might be a worthwhile task to obtain the expert report before pleading the facts to ensure consistency between the report and the pleading. One ought to ensure that the Court's permission to rely on the expert evidence is sought as usual during the proceedings.

CHAPTER NINE

CONCLUDING SUMMARY

When the legal practitioner undertakes the analysis of a case involving foreign immovable property, that analysis should consist of the assessment of three branches under the conflict of laws umbrella.

The first is jurisdiction. Under this branch, the legal practitioner needs to assess whether the Courts of England and Wales hold jurisdiction (the existence of jurisdiction issue) and if so, whether the Courts of England and Wales will likely exercise jurisdiction (the exercise of jurisdiction issue). The starting point on the existence of jurisdiction issue is that the Courts of England and Wales hold no jurisdiction to determine the title to, or the right to possession of, foreign immovable property (i.e. the Moçambique Rule).

However there are three key exceptions. The first is the In Personam Exception which gives the Court jurisdiction to deal with contractual and equitable rights and interests between the parties which may indirectly deal with title to, or right to possession of, foreign immovable property. The second is the Trusts and Estates Exception which gives the Court jurisdiction to deal with a dispute in relation to the administration of a deceased's estate or a trust which consists of a mix of foreign and domestic property and part of that dispute relates to the question of title to, or the right to possession of, foreign property. The third is the Torts Exception which, pursuant to Section 30 (1) of the Civil Jurisdiction and Judgments Act 1982, gives the Court jurisdiction to deal with tortious claims relating to foreign immovable property unless the proceedings are principally concerned with a question of the title to, or the right to possession of, that property. The said question of title or possession has to be the real issue in the proceedings to which any other issue in the case is subordinate.

Nonetheless, even if a jurisdiction exception applies, the legal practitioner must still consult the general additional rules and principles relating to jurisdiction. These general additional rules and principles are wrapped up into the procedural rules on service (CPR Part 6) and challenges to jurisdiction (CPR Part 11). Outside of the specific jurisdictional rules mentioned above, it is the service of proceedings which provides for the existence of the Court's jurisdiction. Defendants can be served within the jurisdiction of England and Wales or, more commonly when dealing with a foreign element, defendants can be served outside of the jurisdiction of England and Wales. If the defendant is to be served outside of the jurisdiction of England and Wales, the claimant must satisfy the Court that (a) there is a good arguable case in relation to a particular gateway contained in paragraph 3.1 of Practice Direction 6B CPR, (b) the claim holds real prospects of success (a serious issue to be tried), (c) England and Wales is clearly and distinctly the most appropriate forum for the trial of the dispute (*forum conveniens*) and (d) in all the circumstances, the Court ought to exercise its ultimate discretion to grant permission to serve out (altogether this deals with the existence and exercise of jurisdiction). Alternatively, a defendant may seek to challenge jurisdiction by application under CPR Part 11 including by applying for a stay of proceedings on the grounds of *forum non conveniens*.

If the jurisdiction branch is satisfied, the legal practitioner must consider the applicable law in relation to the dispute. In the context of contracts related to rights in rem in foreign immovable property the law that applies to the contract will be determined in accordance with the rules contained in the UK Rome I Regulations. If the parties have not chosen the applicable law, the general rule when it comes to contracts dealing with rights in rem in foreign immovable property is that the *lex situs* governs the applicable law of the contract. However, if it can be shown that the contract is manifestly more closely connected with another country, the law of that country will apply to the contract instead. This is a high threshold and exceptional test. Further, the law behind the actual transfer of foreign property interests is governed by the *lex situs*. Once the applicable law is identified, the legal practitioner must ensure the case is suitably presented for the Court. Foreign law must be properly pleaded as a fact in the statements of case and foreign law must be appropriately proven through evidence. This is likely to be by way of expert opinion evidence of a foreign lawyer supported by foreign source material (e.g. foreign statutes and decisions).

The third branch of recognition and enforcement of judgments cannot be forgotten. Whilst outside the scope of this book, the reader will have noted that if the Court's judgment cannot be enforced in the foreign territory, it may refuse jurisdiction and/or refuse to grant the order sought.

This practical guide has intended to provide a route map for a legal practitioner dealing with a case involving foreign immovable property located abroad, particularly in the context of a contractual dispute, setting out some of the main points of jurisdiction and applicable law. As set out earlier, this is not an exhaustive guide and the practitioner ought to consult the main practitioner texts for further and additional details.

MORE BOOKS BY LAW BRIEF PUBLISHING

'The Electronic Communications Code: A Practical Guide – Second Edition' by Kerry Bretherton KC, James Castle, Mark Loveday
'A Practical Guide to the Independent School Standards – September 2023 Edition' by Sarah McKimm
'A Practical Guide to Estate Administration and Crypto Assets' by Richard Marshall
'A Practical Guide to Parental Alienation in Private and Public Law Children Cases' by Sam King QC & Frankie Shama
'Contested Heritage – Removing Art from Land and Historic Buildings' by Richard Harwood QC, Catherine Dobson, David Sawtell
'The Limits of Separate Legal Personality: When Those Running a Company Can Be Held Personally Liable for Losses Caused to Third Parties Outside of the Company' by Dr Mike Wilkinson
'A Practical Guide to Transgender Law' by Robin Moira White & Nicola Newbegin
'A Practical Guide to 'Stranded Spouses' in Family Law' by Mani Singh Basi
'A Practical Guide to Residential Freehold Conveyancing' by Lorraine Richardson
'A Practical Guide to Pensions on Divorce for Lawyers' by Bryan Scant
'A Practical Guide to Challenging Sham Marriage Allegations in Immigration Law' by Priya Solanki
'A Practical Guide to Digital Communications Evidence in Criminal Law' by Sam Willis
'A Practical Guide to Legal Rights in Scotland' by Sarah-Jane Macdonald
'A Practical Guide to New Build Conveyancing' by Paul Sams & Rebecca East
'A Practical Guide to Inherited Wealth on Divorce' by Hayley Trim
'A Practical Guide to Practice Direction 12J and Domestic Abuse in Private Law Children Proceedings' by Rebecca Cross & Malvika Jaganmohan
'A Practical Guide to Confiscation and Restraint' by Narita Bahra QC, John Carl Townsend, David Winch
'A Practical Guide to the Law of Forests in Scotland' by Philip Buchan
'A Practical Guide to Health and Medical Cases in Immigration Law' by Rebecca Chapman & Miranda Butler
'A Practical Guide to Bad Character Evidence for Criminal Practitioners by Aparna Rao
'A Practical Guide to Extradition Law post-Brexit' by Myles Grandison et al
'A Practical Guide to Hoarding and Mental Health for Housing Lawyers' by Rachel Coyle

'Stephens on Contractual Indemnities' by Richard Stephens
'A Practical Guide to the EU Succession Regulation' by Richard Frimston
'A Practical Guide to Solicitor and Client Costs – Second Edition' by Robin Dunne
'Constructive Dismissal – Practice Pointers and Principles' by Benjimin Burgher
'A Practical Guide to Religion and Belief Discrimination Claims in the Workplace' by Kashif Ali
'A Practical Guide to the Law of Medical Treatment Decisions' by Ben Troke
'Fundamental Dishonesty and QOCS in Personal Injury Proceedings: Law and Practice' by Jake Rowley
'A Practical Guide to the Law in Relation to School Exclusions' by Charlotte Hadfield & Alice de Coverley
'A Practical Guide to Divorce for the Silver Separators' by Karin Walker
'The Right to be Forgotten – The Law and Practical Issues' by Melissa Stock
'A Practical Guide to Planning Law and Rights of Way in National Parks, the Broads and AONBs' by James Maurici QC, James Neill et al
'A Practical Guide to Election Law' by Tom Tabori
'A Practical Guide to the Law in Relation to Surrogacy' by Andrew Powell
'A Practical Guide to Claims Arising from Fatal Accidents – Second Edition' by James Patience
'A Practical Guide to Asbestos Claims' by Jonathan Owen & Gareth McAloon
'A Practical Guide to Stamp Duty Land Tax in England and Northern Ireland' by Suzanne O'Hara
'A Practical Guide to the Law of Farming Partnerships' by Philip Whitcomb
'A Practical Guide to the Law of Unlawful Eviction and Harassment – Second Edition' by Stephanie Lovegrove
'A Practical Guide to Costs in Personal Injury Claims – Second Edition' by Matthew Hoe
'A Practical Guide to the General Data Protection Regulation (GDPR) – Second Edition' by Keith Markham
'A Practical Guide to Working with Litigants in Person and McKenzie Friends in Family Cases' by Stuart Barlow
'Protecting Unregistered Brands: A Practical Guide to the Law of Passing Off' by Lorna Brazell
'A Practical Guide to Secondary Liability and Joint Enterprise Post-Jogee' by Joanne Cecil & James Mehigan

'A Practical Guide to the Pre-Action RTA Claims Protocol for Personal Injury Lawyers' by Antonia Ford
'A Practical Guide to Neighbour Disputes and the Law' by Alexander Walsh
'A Practical Guide to Coercive Control for Legal Practitioners and Victims' by Rachel Horman
'A Practical Guide to the Law of Driverless Cars – Second Edition'
by Alex Glassbrook, Emma Northey & Scarlett Milligan
'A Practical Guide to TOLATA Claims' by Greg Williams
'A Practical Guide to Elderly Law – Second Edition' by Justin Patten
'A Practical Guide to Responding to Housing Disrepair and Unfitness Claims' by Iain Wightwick
'A Practical Guide to the Law of Bullying and Harassment in the Workplace' by Philip Hyland
'How to Be a Freelance Solicitor: A Practical Guide to the SRA-Regulated Freelance Solicitor Model' by Paul Bennett
'A Practical Guide to Prison Injury Claims' by Malcolm Johnson
'A Practical Guide to Advising Clients at the Police Station' by Colin Stephen McKeown-Beaumont
'A Practical Guide to Antisocial Behaviour Injunctions – Second Edition' by Iain Wightwick
'Practical Mediation: A Guide for Mediators, Advocates, Advisers, Lawyers, and Students in Civil, Commercial, Business, Property, Workplace, and Employment Cases' by Jonathan Dingle with John Sephton
'The Mini-Pupillage Workbook' by David Boyle
'A Practical Guide to Crofting Law' by Brian Inkster
'A Practical Guide to the Law of Domain Names and Cybersquatting' by Andrew Clemson
'A Practical Guide to the Law of Gender Pay Gap Reporting' by Harini Iyengar
'NHS Whistleblowing and the Law' by Joseph England
'Employment Law and the Gig Economy' by Nigel Mackay & Annie Powell
'A Practical Guide to Noise Induced Hearing Loss (NIHL) Claims' by Andrew Mckie, Ian Skeate, Gareth McAloon
'An Introduction to Beauty Negligence Claims – A Practical Guide for the Personal Injury Practitioner' by Greg Almond
'Intercompany Agreements for Transfer Pricing Compliance' by Paul Sutton
'Zen and the Art of Mediation' by Martin Plowman
'A Practical Guide to Adoption for Family Lawyers' by Graham Pegg

'A Practical Guide to Industrial Disease Claims' by Andrew Mckie & Ian Skeate
'A Practical Guide to Conducting a Sheriff Court Proof' by Andrew Stevenson
'A Practical Guide to Vicarious Liability' by Mariel Irvine
'A Practical Guide to Applications for Landlord's Consent and Variation of Leases' by Mark Shelton
'A Practical Guide to Relief from Sanctions Post-Mitchell and Denton' by Peter Causton
'A Practical Guide to Equity Release for Advisors' by Paul Sams
'A Practical Guide to Financial Services Claims' by Chris Hegarty
'A Practical Guide to Financial Ombudsman Service Claims' by Adam Temple & Robert Scrivenor
'A Practical Guide to Running Housing Disrepair and Cavity Wall Claims – Second Edition' by Andrew Mckie & Ian Skeate
'A Practical Guide to Holiday Sickness Claims – Second Edition' by Andrew Mckie & Ian Skeate
'Arguments and Tactics for Personal Injury and Clinical Negligence Claims' by Dorian Williams
'A Practical Guide to Drone Law' by Rufus Ballaster, Andrew Firman, Eleanor Clot
'On Experts: CPR35 for Lawyers and Experts' by David Boyle
'An Introduction to Personal Injury Law' by David Boyle

These books and more are available to order online direct from the publisher at www.lawbriefpublishing.com, where you can also read free sample chapters. For any queries, call us on 0844 587 2383 or email us at mail@lawbriefpublishing.com.

Our books are all generally in stock at www.amazon.co.uk with free next day delivery for Prime members, and at good legal bookshops such as Wildy & Sons.

We are regularly launching new books in our series of practical day-to-day practitioners' guides. Visit our website and join our free newsletter to be kept informed and to receive special offers, free chapters, etc.

You can also follow us on Twitter at www.twitter.com/lawbriefpub.

www.ingramcontent.com/pod-product-compliance
Lightning Source LLC
LaVergne TN
LVHW022311200926
848481LV00004B/1285